CONTEMPLATIVE REALISM:

A THEOLOGICAL-AESTHETICAL MANIFESTO

JOSHUA HREN

BENEDICT XVI
+—INSTITUTE—+
FOR SACRED MUSIC AND DIVINE WORSHIP

For Michael D. O'Brien,

στη φιλία

. . . *the mystery is not a secret here; it is, on the contrary, something that is said and manifested.*

—Giorgio Agamben

Realists do not fear the results of their study.

—Dostoevsky

CONTEMPLATIVE REALISM
A THEOLOGICAL-AESTHETICAL MANIFESTO

As ever, but especially in our present age of raging post-truth unreality, we ought to heed the Holy Father's summons to "ask rather more carefully what 'the real' actually is." To ignore the question is to risk settling for a life seen through a limited lens that cannot grasp truth's terrible splendor. To remain indifferent could drive us to counterfeit the Book of Creation, and so to falsify human and divine being.

Realism—from Flaubert and Henry James to Willa Cather ("Realism is a protest against lies," she wrote), to Jonathan Franzen in our own day—has gifted literature and its readers with considerable gains. With its insistence upon exacting explorations of characters' psychological contours, with its willingness to countenance difficulties and tragedies and move beyond the novel's youthful proclivity towards sentimentality, realism commits us to increasing what James calls the "felt life" that exists in the story by *telling the hard-won truth* instead of handing out rosy romances.

But so-called "realism," when relegated to material tangibilities, can blind us—instead of binding us—to things as they are. In his *Spirit of the Liturgy*, Pope Benedict XVI prophecies against such myopic mediocrity. "Are we not interested in the cosmos anymore?" Benedict asks. "Are we today really hopelessly huddled in our own little circle? Is it not important, precisely today, to pray with the whole of creation?" We who were born under the halogen star of secularism, who from birth have been initiated into the cults of health and consumerist titillation, can come all too unconsciously to live as though there is no unseen, no afterlife destiny, as if our souls were mere brain matter, knowable via fine-tuned microscopes and mendable through the proper chemicals. Or perhaps we preserve a cellar of our souls for angels and demons and heaven and hell, but these intangibles become peripheral, spurious sideshows, shadows darkened by the technicolor liturgies of late liberal life. Gnawed by an unnoticed *acedia*, too many believers worship with slumped posture—treating the alternate time of the liturgical calendar as an impotent interruption of our "busy schedules," turning churches into bourgeois living rooms. Rose windows are replaced by big screens onto which the people of God are invited to project therapeutic fantasies of a sentimentalized piety. With Pope Benedict we can't help but wonder: does anyone *really* rest easily on the supposedly solid ground of such a circumscribed cosmos?" If this preeminent mind of our time is not wrong, and "the man who puts to one side the reality of God is a realist only in appearance," then we ought to ask with unflinching intensity and absolute openness: what is real?

Like liturgy, literature asks this question, distinct in its depth from the flippancy of Pilate's sophistic "what is truth?", with a range of forms that answer it very differently. At times both art and worship seem to devolve into the manners and mood of self-referential and inconsequential play, gestures without meaning, or "bank notes" (says Benedict) "without funds to cover them." These too-closed circles of communication wall off transcendence. In living cruciform liturgy—on the contrary—"the congregation does not offer its own thoughts or poetry but is taken out of itself and given the privilege of sharing in the cosmic song of praise of the cherubim and seraphim." In living literature something analogous happens: we suffer and praise with the whole of creation; the prose cultivates a grateful disposition, prompting us to yearn for a vision of the whole. "To experience the beautiful is not only to be satisfied," John Milbank aptly argues, "but also to be frustrated satisfyingly; a desire to see more of what arrives

. . . is always involved." From the quest for eternal life in *The Epic of Gilgamesh* to the interplanetary paradise of Dante's *Divine Comedy*; from Odysseus' conversations with the dead's ghouls in Hades to the profitable sales of deceased serfs in Nikolai Gogol's *Dead Souls*; from Dostoevsky's zealously-otherworldly "Dream of a Ridiculous Man" to the mass-media miracle that culminates Don DeLillo's *Underworld*, literature has been asking us to answer this question: what is real?

So. Let's get real. By this year of our Lord so many species of realism have cropped up that to introduce another one could seem vanity of vanities in the funhouse of fiction. I would almost call the endeavor *hysterical*, were it not the case that former *New Yorker* editor James Wood has already made "hysterical realism" a live category. We receive novelist Zadie Smith's reproof of Wood as a fair warning against any critical taxonomy or manifesto, instantiations of which will inevitably—and often blessedly—depart from its foundational features: "any collective term for a supposed literary movement," Smith tells us, "is always too large a net, catching significant dolphins among so much cannable tuna." For reasons of convenience, and on account of, well, general mortality, I shall trot out "the contemplative realist" as if he were a single literary denizen, sacrificing singularities for the sake of what contemplative realists hold in common. Wood rightly relates that nearly every major literary movement in the past few centuries has consciously sought to see and say "the way things are," even as "the definition of what is 'realistic' changes." These genealogical metamorphoses lead some (such as Roland Barthes) to proclaim that "realism does not refer to reality; realism is not realistic."

But this manifesto on behalf of a "contemplative realism" makes no claims to create, *ex nihilo*, a new aesthetical species. Nor does it advance this rough school of literary fish as some preeminent or sole "way forward" for fiction in our time. Rather, it seeks to articulate a literary approach that exists already in diffuse books and also in the potencies of living artists. It seeks to gather and galvanize those souls. More than anything, it yearns to quicken a contemplative realist disposition among as many comers as possible—literary chops or no. What Bernanos so ably argued all those years ago has, unfortunately, only gained in truthfulness: "we can witness a lethal slackening of men's conscience that is attacking not only their moral life, but also their very heart and mind, altering and decomposing even their imagination . . . the menacing crisis is one of infantilism." In a very bad way (to borrow from Josef Pieper), "man's ability to *see* is in decline."

One reason it is in decline is that human beings have come to see reality itself as a construct—a cacophony of constantly changing conventions. Discarded is St. Thomas' definition of truth as the "adequation of mind to reality." But as Wood and so many others posit, reality changes according to the era: he seems to mean "cultural and social reality," sets of conventions which may be rightly said to shift. There is no stable real to which the mind can conform itself. Now, there is no question that human nature is alternately pressured and stretched, shaped and malformed by various social conventions. The inhabitant of ancient Athens and the denizen of a technocracy, each under the influence of their social situation, will be directed towards various conventional ends which are now closer and now farther from their natural ends. This is what Peter Maurin meant when he worked "to make that kind of society where it is easier for men to be good." He was not preaching utopia. The contemplative realist recognizes the ways in which convention and nature are in harmony or at war in the situation of his story. He finds in these discrepancies a skyscraper full of dramatic tension.

The accidents of actuality are always changing. But, as Katy Carl notes, "Wood either passes over as irrelevant, or prescinds from as unknowable, anything we might call 'human nature' or even 'nature' stably defined." Yes, Wood goes so far as to dismiss "Nature" as a "category beloved of neoclassical critics, the overwhelmingly strong Aristotelian tradition with its distinction between probability and the improbably marvelous." He calls into question the claims of Wordsworth and Coleridge that literature can offer "a natural delineation of human passions, human characters, and human incidents." As Adrian Vermeule argues, those who deny an innate nature treat the human being as "a blank scroll on which the autonomous individual will can write whatever life plan it pleases," seeing "the human body itself as a plastic mold to be formed through surgical modification into whatever shape or age or gender the body's gnostic inhabitant fancies—the anthropological equivalent of corporate strip-mining that ruins the natural landscape in the name of economic utility." By contrast, the contemplative realist adheres to the stability of both nature and human nature, seeing both as created by God and the latter as particularly defined by the interplay between the tripartite human faculties of intellect, will, and appetites (or passions), all of which can be conveyed through characters' movement from potency to actuality as well as their regression from actualization to impotence. In his commentary on Aristotle's *Poetics,* Francis Ferguson rightly explains that though willed action and suffered passions are "abstractly considered . . . opposites . . . in our human experience action and passion are always combined."

Virginia Woolf announces the modernist's commitment to a putative instability of nature when she quips that "On or around December 1910, human character changed. I am not saying that one went out, as one might into a garden, and there saw that a rose had flowered or a hen had laid an egg. The change was not sudden and definite like that, but a change there was, nevertheless . . ." The contemplative realist appreciates the humor here, but rejects the philosophical premise. Woolf was closer to the mark when, in "The Narrow Bridge of Art," she wondered over the riddles of humanity: "the mind is full of monstrous, hybrid, unmanageable emotions" (though we might clarify the point: unmanageable as our emotions may be, they can be resisted; they do not *define* us). The contemplative realist assents, also, to Woolf's observation that "human life lasts but a second; that the capacity of the human mind is nevertheless boundless; that life is infinitely beautiful yet repulsive." Human nature is certainly broad. At this fact Dmitri Karamazov balks: "No, man is broad, even too broad, I would narrow him down." But the contemplative realist knows that we must take things as they are: man is capable of "the Madonna" and "Sodom," holiness and hell-bent viciousness: humankind has a *telos* toward the Good and a concupiscent talent for mucking up that trajectory and there is nothing we can do, existentially speaking, about either. We must accept our shared plight without cynicism, at times suffering our characters' indiscretions without forfeiting hope, at others following them toward heights we ourselves may fail to reach.

Nature too, though riddled with vestiges of God, is also marred by fissures. The contemplative realist does not fail to countenance the challenge Benjamin Myers throws out with all the soul-searing luminosity of a firebrand:

The Reverend on Natural Theology

Seeing God in nature do
you see Him crucified? The rabbit ripped
by dogs, its guts strewn across a crew-
cut field, the hide left wet where it was stripped?
Driving through countryside you sometimes see

a line of coyote pelts hung from barbed fence,
flapped by high wind, bothered with flies and flea
infested, bullet holes in all the skins.
Do you then read the Book of Nature's red
ink dribbled down the posts? Consider all
the world's wide gore, the white-tailed deer that's spread
across the road, the earth's unlapped offal.
Everything broken must be broken again.
I will make you fissures of men.

If nature croons with beauty it also groans for redemption, twitching under the fierce jaws of necessity. One is reminded of a letter the exiled poet Czeslaw Milosz wrote to the troubled monk Thomas Merton:

> Every time you speak of Nature, it appears to you as soothing, rich in symbols, as a veil or curtain. You do not pay much attention to torture or suffering in Nature . . . We live through a time when Manichaeism is particularly strong and one could enumerate many reasons for it—though we do not grasp as yet all the causes. I do not know to what extent a sort of despair at the sight of ruthless necessity in Nature is justified. Yet it exists while it was not known until quite modern times. The distance between man and the rest of Creation was so great that for Descartes too the animal was a machine. Some old Manichaean elements started to revive perhaps in the Reformation but they were mitigated. You can say that overstressed compassion for millions and billions of creatures crushed every second makes part of the modern schism which destroyed quite real barriers between man and animal.

Willa Cather exemplifies a truthful tension familiar to the realistic contemplative. In her novel *Death Comes for the Archbishop*, nature contains "geometrical nightmares"; not all the created world is immediately beautiful, and some of it is kind of overwhelming and scary, but then its sublimity has a primordial capacity to bring us to silent gratitude and awe—as when Father Latour, lost in the missionary desert, encounters a "cruciform tree" in an hour of need. How few novels and novelists hold these disparate characteristics of nature in tension: there is so much room for the novel to move in that direction.

The contemplative realist invites us to be bothered by our hapless treatment of nature as mere spectacle, resistant to portraits of nature as soothing anodyne, and yet certain that a right sight of nature, with all its own tortures and sufferings, will correct the pantheistic compassion and the algebraic abstraction of Modernity.

Pieper provides us with a description and definition of that contemplation which we so badly need as an antidote for this prevalent decline. Contemplation connotes, quite simply, "seeing, beholding, perceiving some reality." More precisely, it is an "attitude of receptive observation." That particular artist whom I wish to call the contemplative realist must, in Pieper's words, "be endowed with the ability to see in an exceptionally intensive manner." Meticulously, intensely, he stores up in his heart a fullness of perception which pours out on the page not what everybody sees but rather "what not everybody sees." Here is no abstract art, indifferent to the contours of the concrete and visible world. Nor are we dealing with a "merely descriptive realism." What Pieper applies to his ideal sculptor we would do well to aspire after in prose: "nothing in this affirming closeness to reality smacks of false idealization, nothing is embellished as if all reality were wholesome and without rough edges." Only the loving gaze (*ubi amor, ibi oculus*) can contemplate fully, for "a new dimension of 'seeing' is opened up by love alone." A lover can never "see enough," Pieper writes—"the desire to 'see enough' is never satisfied." It is an essential fact of contemplative realism that the desire to really see is necessarily unfulfilled.

If St. John Henry Newman was not wrong to define literature as the "study of human nature," this focus on human beings ignores the painterly noticing that the novel developed—that inclination to pause and—more than merely "set the stage" for the characters—celebrate the beautiful background so fully that its significance becomes nearly as important as human action. This painterly attentiveness is a central attribute of contemplative realism.

Joseph Conrad gives a partial portrait of the contemplative realist when, in his famous Preface, he imagines an artist who reaches beyond the noise and struggle of existence into our "less obvious capacities," knowing that there is a "vulnerable body within a steel armor. His appeal is less loud, more profound, less distinct, more stirring," and he "speaks to our capacity for delight and wonder, to the sense of mystery surrounding our lives." He does this by conveying the "invincible conviction of solidarity" that binds "the dead to the living and the living to the unborn." He does so in prose that stimulates our senses, yes, but with an "unswerving devotion to the perfect blending of form and substance," a feat the artist can only achieve "through an unremitting, never-discouraged care for the shape and ring of sentences." Only through this careful, contemplative devotion will the realist manifest that "light of magic suggestiveness . . . for an evanescent instant over the commonplace surface of words," words which have been "defaced by ages of careless usage."

Conrad's passage captures the hard fact that earthly

contemplation is far from perfect. As Pieper puts it, "in the midst of its repose there is unrest. This unrest stems from man's experiencing at one and the same moment the overwhelming infinitude of the object, and his own limitations." Romano Guardini gets at this in "The Meaning of Melancholy" when he depicts the artistic temperament's pained epiphany that what needs to be said and shown is past realization, revealing that "death is the neighbor of the beautiful." Every little death, every phrase that falls short, every unwritten novel can tempt the artist to an evil melancholy consisting of the "consciousness that the eternal did not attain the form intended for it." But these imperfections can also usher in undulating gratitude for whatever iotas have bespoke the eternal, in whatever necessarily elliptical way. By its nature, earthly contemplation spies a light whose surpassing eloquence blinds and graces us both.

What does it mean to say that the contemplative is also a "realist," a realist who, per Dostoevsky, "does not fear the results of his study"?

In his mesmerizing classic *Mimesis,* Erich Auerbach argues that literary realism reached its apogee with Flaubert's *Madame Bovary.* Flaubert's realism breathes most meaningfully in an everyday scene of a commonplace meal: Charles and Emma sit at a table without a cloth. The smell of boiled beef brings her near despair. Her husband is a slow eater. Emma "would amuse herself making marks on the oilcloth with the point of her table knife." For Flaubert, the self-effacing artist could represent such a scene so "purely and completely" that "it interprets itself" far more realistically than if the author were to interfere with appended judgments or opinions. In place of a romantic writer's "grandiloquent and ostentatious parading of the writer's own feelings," Flaubert exemplified the art of "self-forgetful absorption in the subjects of reality which transforms them and permits them to develop to mature expression." On the one hand, Auerbach admits, realism could be considered "objective seriousness," the effort to reach into the depths of human passions without the prose betraying the artist's own arguments. On the other, in spite of his ambitions to avoid "taking of sides," the assertions of Flaubert's own style over unfiltered actuality leads to a "didactic purpose: criticism of the contemporary world."

This criticism did not spare satirical portraits of subscribers to species of "enlightened" scientism, but the unsparing critique of all illusions hounded Flaubert's depiction of religion also: Emma Bovary's religious phases are simply another variety of subjective and romantic escapism; the Bovarys' priest is an all-too-human pusillanimous man, blind to his pettiness and utter carnality because his clerical spectacles distort any chance to see things as they are. Flaubertian realism's dictum that we must "take things as they are" (resisting "oughts" as wishful, delusional) assigns a circumscribed meaning to that *as they are*: What "is" is, for the materialist-realist, only that which can be seen; the unseen is taken to be unreal.

When Henry James called Flaubert a "Benedictine of the actual" he must have meant, in part, that actual Benedictines contemplate the unreal, whereas literary realists take that ascetical devotion and aim it at things "as they are"—as they can be seen, touched, heard, smelled, tasted—intuited, too, up to a certain point but not past it. Flaubertian realism treats of the spiritual aspects of human life with a skepticism that is, for the contemplative realist, needlessly restrictive in its diet.

Vladimir Nabokov typifies the consequences of this reduction in his dismissal of "all the fantastic tales as juvenilia"; as Richard Pevear notes, for Nabokov "the real Gogol" included only "The Overcoat" and other such stories which purportedly portray the "shadows of other worlds" as passing "like the shadows of nameless and soundless ships." For the *real* Gogol, on the contrary, "the fantastic and the diabolical were always essential dimensions of this world." Boris Eichenbaum gets at this dynamic when he resists the supposed "incomprehensible intrusion of 'romanticism' into 'realism'" at the end of "The Overcoat," when the poor clerk Akaky Akakievich persists on the pages after his death, as policemen and nocturnal walkers see with their own eyes an indubitable phantom of the dead man, albeit "much taller now" and with "an enormous mustache."

Notice the deadpan, seamless seriousness with which the comically realist face is rendered—specific details doing their duty to realistically portray the dead man. There is no clear dichotomy between the initial "realism" exploring the travails of a petty worker and the "fantastic" ghost-filled finish: rather, the end of the tale "emerges into a world of more usual concepts and facts, but everything is treated in the style of playing with fantasy." To be clear, in its fullest expressions, contemplative realism, contrary to its cousin "magical realism," distances itself from "fantasy" or "magic" altogether—distances itself in its own aesthetic execution while appreciating fantasy wholeheartedly as legit in its own right; Thomas Mirus is on to something when he reads the flourishing of fantasy as one of many signs that regular realism is a kind of literary aberration rather than a rule. As Matthew Strecher explains, magical realism is "what happens when a highly detailed, realistic setting is invaded by something too strange to believe." Whereas magical realism combines a fully-fleshed out mundane world with fantastical, magical elements that are at odds with the commonplace characters and their secular world, contemplative realism registers the supernatural as harmonious with the natural, a poetic extension of the Thomistic understanding that though it may *feel* as if grace grates against nature, in truth God's movements build upon it.

Still more, whereas magical realism not infrequently relishes the ambiguous, contemplative realism favors mystery over ambiguity. In that classic tale of magical realism, "A Very Old Man with Enormous Wings," the great Colombian fictionist Gabriel García Márquez gives us a flurry of interpretations as to what the titular character might be, but resists a conclusive identification of his nature, seemingly in order to espouse a posture of skeptical uncertainty. There is no question that the universe is riddled with mystery. As G.K. Chesterton diagnoses it, "Mysticism keeps men sane. As long as you have mystery you have health; when you destroy mystery you create morbidity. The ordinary man has always been sane because the ordinary man has always been a mystic. He has permitted the twilight. He has always had one foot in earth and the other in fairyland." Mystery as an element amidst other intelligible things is one thing; to foster ambiguity as a fundamental premise or "position" towards all of reality—this is something else entirely. Mystery invites intrigue combined with intensive musing ordered toward the real possibility of at least partial answers; when answers fail to arrive, the acolyte of mystery submits in humility. Applied as a principle, ambiguity projects twilight where truth can be told and suspends meaning by careful design; novels built on this foundation of quickening sand take ambiguous endings as their necessary telos. Contemplative realists may plant apparent ambiguities at the start of their stories, but as their arcs unfold these tales reveal meaning. There are plenty of ways in which ambiguities can be beneficially incorporated into a story as one device among many (unreliable narration, most obviously, or the ambivalent gestures of a character, or double-entendre dialogue). There is no reason why a story cannot end without every mystery having been solved; some suspension of meaning is merely a reflection of the straw-grasping limitations of being human. But even in cases wherein the truth is troubled, not fully tallied and divvied, the contemplative realist will always leave the reader firmly reciting the indispensable *X-Files* mantra: "The truth is out there."

This effect, as accomplished in Eugene Vodolazkin's novel *Laurus*, stretches like a tightrope between nature and supernature. Mystery in that novel gathers cumulatively, so much so that any single example can hardly do it justice. It may seem at first that we are reading a magical realist work when an early line explains that, in a forest beside the ruins of the main characters' church centuries after the novel's main action, "apparations chat up mushroom pickers from time to time." Yet unlike the immersive peculiarities of *One Hundred Years of Solitude*, the singularities in *Laurus* gather slowly and consist mainly of matter-of-fact, doubt-free assertions that presence spiritual realities: angels, human spirits, the immaterial reality of death itself which at one point leads away a soul "by the hand" and pats it "on the cheek." The soul in this scene is depicted as

> small, almost childlike. Her response to the affectionate gesture was more likely fear than gratitude. This is how children respond to those who take them from their kin for an indefinite period: life (death) for them will, perhaps, not be bad, but it will be completely different from what they are used to, lacking the former structure, familiar events, and turns of speech. As they leave, they keep looking back and seeing their frightened reflections in the teary eyes of their kin.

Meanwhile the novel's physical world hews closely to the naturalistic, never becoming itself fantastic but insisting that what cannot be seen is as realistic as what can, even if the former is "almost translucent and thus inconspicuous." This presencing transcends the merely aesthetic. Though in the early stages of the novel a reader wishing for distance from Christofer and Arseny's single-entendre faith may be able to hold aloof, saying that its expression is a mere function of their historical circumstance, by the conclusion it becomes undeniable that the reader needs to make a decision: How much uncomplicated credence can be lent to events such as those being presented for our acceptance? As Vodolazkin tiptoes across the uncanny tightrope joining the seemingly impossible and the narratively undeniable, the firmness of his grounding in nature and human nature permit us to hope, too, in his depiction of the unironically and unambiguously supernatural.

(.)

The contemplative realist aesthetic is analogous to the aspect of sacred Scripture St. Augustine examines in *On Christian Teaching*. Why, he wonders, did God admit so many apparent ambiguities—so many mysteries—into Divine Revelation? "I do not doubt," he hazards, "that this was divinely arranged for the purpose of subduing pride by toil, and of preventing a feeling of satiety in the intellect, which generally holds in small esteem what is discovered without difficulty." Difficult passages in texts function as a sort of blessed puzzle, activating the intellect and imagination and rewarding contemplative exertion. Against the reams of unread dissertations the prosecution will haul out as testament, in spite of the fact that during certain decades *Ulysses* might just have had more peer-reviewed articles plumbing its pages than *The Book of Job,* fiction does not merit the degree of study Sacred Scripture does. Henry James' story "The Figure in the Carpet" comically pokes fun at critics who take "supersubtle" fiction as a sort of Holy Book whose hidden meanings are arranged like "a complex figure in a Persian carpet;" the great "secret" drives the critics mad, and no "Eureka!" rescues them from their appetite for an Answer.

Other inhabitants of realism leave more room for the "supernatural," so long as the story makes clear that what we name by that appellation is in fact the numinous depths of our own psyches: God, or the gods, Satan and the demons, phantoms of all shapes, are, under this view, projections. Even as Virginia Woolf distances herself from slavish realism ("Why should a real chair be better than an imaginary elephant?"), she set a limit to the terrain of what the modern reader would tolerate. Woolf defended even the ghosts of Henry James, another "founding father" of realism, because they "have nothing in common with the violent old ghosts—the bloodstained sea captains, the white horses, the headless ladies of dark lanes and windy commons. They have their origin within us." Tempted at first to believe that the ghost in *The Turn of the Screw* is real, we sober up, but the startled state is still unnerving, for "We are afraid of something, perhaps, in ourselves. In short, we turn on the light." James, that courtly, delicate old soul, "can still make us afraid of the dark."

The unresolvable numinous is the mood belief assumes in most modern fiction: supposedly spiritual happenings are rendered with a relativized suspension of disbelief, reflecting only a notional indulgence in firm, unironic, simple-hearted credulity. Ron Hansen's lyrically beautiful *Mariette in Ecstasy* exemplifies this approach: the protagonist may be a misguided and unstable adolescent, or she may be an authentic mystic: the text will bear either reading equally well, so that while the conclusion satisfies on an aesthetic level, it leaves behind an aftertaste of craving for certitude. Although Hansen himself may have childlike faith in the realities of Christian mysticism, the reader is denied certainty about Mariette's position with regard to those realities. The distance is only a stone's throw from Woolf's supernatural solipsism to this aesthetics of Christian subjectivism, even as the latter at least leaves room for union with a God not of our making.

To be sure, though materialist realism retains many adherents, it has also roused some formidable discontents. Dostoevsky called himself a realist "in a higher sense." J.K. Huysmans, the decadent convert to Catholicism, coined the term "supernatural realism." In *The Damned*, Huysmans' thinly-veiled messenger Durtal muses on Grünewald's paintings of Christ, calling the painter "the most uncompromising of realists":

> but to regard this redeemer of the doss-house, this God of the morgue, was an inspirational experience. A gleam of light filtered from the ulcerated head; a superhuman expression illuminated the gangrened flesh and the convulsed features. This crucified corpse was truly that of a God, and, without aureole, without nimbus, with only the blood-sprinkled crown of thorns for accoutrement.

In his own tormented and sensory-spiritual prose, Huysmans does for the novel what Grünewald did for painting: he "extracted the very essence of charity and despair" from the "triumphant depths of squalor," and ushered in an art "ordained to render the invisible and the intangible." This aesthetics has a name: "supernatural realism."

In Huysman's characterization we sense the subtext of realism-as-gritty-underbelly, an affiliation of the horrible as the somehow "more real" brought to bear on Christ himself, especially in the illumined gangrene. Here, the supernatural exists in a sort of antagonistic tension with the real rudeness of nature. We find an urban analogy to this tension in Mikhail Bakhtin's description, in *Problems of Dostoevsky's Poetics*, of Dosty's organic, fantastic manner of combining "a mystical-religious element with an extreme" and even crude "slum naturalism," wherein the "adventures of truth on earth" take place in dens of thieves and taverns, marketplaces and prisons. Other artists settle for naturalism that is both starved of the supernatural and eager to rub harsh realities in our rapt faces. Dietrich von Hildebrand calls out the formal and spiritual poverty of art that "breathes out upon us all the depressing triviality of this milieu." In such works, the wretchedness of the earth is wrought with the "intensive effect of barrenness being diffused." Whereas genuine art "transposes" even the harshest parts of reality in a way that resists oppressive and restrictive characterization, in naturalistic depiction the "metaphysical ugliness of that which is depicted destroys the true artistic beauty." This insistence that the real is most honestly congealed in the overbearingly ugliness of being amounts to a denial of nature's irrevocable goodness. But nature is not all that is lost in such literature. "The real" here is taken to exclude the supernatural shattering instantiated through those same slums, those "dark holes of the poor" where St. Teresa of Calcutta prayed her Hail Marys beside the deathbed gutters.

But for materialist realists truth is not something that adventures *through* the mire and the muck: it *is* the yuck that we'd prefer to pretend away. The association of realism with the ugly and unpleasant but accurate truth finds a political parallel in the *realpolitik* of Machiavelli, who considered it sensible to "go straight to a discussion of how things are in real life," for his predecessors, with their predilection for imagined republics, promise fantasies and deliver pain. Why? Because "the gap between how people actually behave and how they ought to behave is so great that anyone who ignores everyday reality in order to live up to an ideal will soon discover he has been taught how to destroy himself, not how to preserve himself." In practice, however, Machiavelli executes a severely limited depiction of what counts as reality—in political life or outside of it. As Pierre Manent points out, Machiavelli convinces us to "fix our attention exclusively, or almost exclusively, on pathologies. He wants us to lose what, after having read him, we shall be tempted to call our 'innocence.'" He cultivated suspicion strategically in order to persuade us that whatever "good" we possess is premised upon necessary evils.

Transposed into a psychological key, Manent comes close to narrating what Jonathan Franzen calls "depressive realism"—that supposedly sobering reminder that "You are, after all, just protoplasm, and some day you'll be dead." We can share Franzen's applause of this realism's radical critique of "therapeutic society," while remaining, as he does, discontent with the depressive's dubious divination that the world is really rotten. In his essay "Why Bother?", Franzen wonders whether this sort of realism isn't merely a "mask" for depression's true essence, which is "an overwhelming estrangement from humanity"—and, the contemplative realist can't help but add—from the felt presence of God. In an effort to overcome the immobilizing tyranny of depressive realism, Franzen fosters what he calls a "tragic realism," which "preserves access to the dirt behind the dream of [political-theological] Chosenness—to the human difficulty beneath the technological ease, to the sorrow behind the pop-cultural narcosis: to all those portents on the margins of our existence." The contemplative realist concedes Franzen's claim that "improvement always comes at a cost" (though we call this the lie of "cheap grace"), and that unalloyed goodness is rarer than badness and evil—at least in the heart of man. Franzen finds a philosophical foundation for his aesthetic in Nietzsche's powerful work *The Birth of Tragedy*, which accuses Christianity of dealing death to the Greeks' glorious embrace of Dionysian darkness: "From its very outset," he chides, "Christianity was . . . a feeling which merely disgusted, hid and decked itself out in its belief in a 'another' or 'better' life . . . a Beyond, invented in order better to defame the Here-and-Now." The contemplative realist concedes Nietzsche's central insight that narratives bless us by granting Apollonian beauty, clarity, and form to human hardships that are anarchic, dark, Dionysian. He nods his head fervently to Franzen's assurance that "the formal aesthetic rendering of the human plight can be (though I'm afraid we novelists are rightly mocked for overusing the word) redemptive."

While all human life will ultimately be judged according to Christ, in fiction it would be dishonest to force eucatastrophe out of every complication: some genuine goods can sear through our encounter with decent but flawed people, with troubled, imperfect characters of good will whose self-destructive decisions and dire situations draw them close to hell's gates. Artists who render this trajectory for us do us a great service—often purging us, through catharsis, of temptations which we share with their protagonists. Sins can lose their lure when we see characters act out immoralities we only imagined.

In *Christ and Apollo*, William F. Lynch helpfully discriminates between a "dishonest" tragedy, which gloats and even demonaically guffaws over our helplessness, and a mode of tragedy that holds in tension the noble potentialities of humanity with the depths of pain and loss to which we can descend. When tragedy "is really achieved" through the "great tragic texts," we are brought to an "experience of deep beauty and exaltation, but not by way of beauty and exaltation." Catholic writers can employ a tragic key insofar as tragedy is "rooted in mystical conquests of the human spirit over pain, in the emergence of godlike strength and qualities in man in the very midst of tragic defeat."

True, on the deepest level of existence, the Christian must unite his agonies with those of the all-sufficient Master, knowing with St. Paul that we can "fill up those things that are wanting of the sufferings of Christ, in my flesh, for his body, which is the church" (Cols 1:24, DV). And yet, as fiction that tracks conversions can help us grasp, the human spirit frequently dies "in real helplessness," to use Lynch's language.

However, this "really tragic level of existence," he explains, "is the region of the soul into which Christianity descends in order to operate its unique effects. . . . There is a point to which the mind must come where it realizes it is no match for the full mystery of existence, where, therefore, it suffers a death." Often it is only fully here, from this posture, that we fully consent to put on the mind of God—to surrender to Christ's redemptive suffering—"and thus rise to a higher knowledge and insight." Here, at this point, death and life coincide in a single act, and "in this sense Christian faith has the tragic at its very core"; it is always "an extremely complicated mixture of dying and living; at no stage in the whole life of faith can death be screened out."

Franzen cites Flannery O'Connor, who argues that "People without hope not only don't write novels, but what is more to the point, they don't read them," but when the tragic realist countenances the most abysmal shades of darkness, what will give him the necessary hope to surface again and tell the tale? One of the tasks, then, of the contemplative realist, is to loosen tragedy from its inner-ressentiment, its prospective disgust and cynical gloating over our infinite absurdities—its "depressive realism."

Any number of literary realisms dramatize and induce a wariness that is one part Machiavelli, one part Nietzsche, and one part Freud. As Jorge Luis Borges argues, the reader of detective fiction (a type of reader Poe "created") approaches stories "with incredulity and suspicions." Not only is nothing as it seems, but what seemed to be good turns out to be filled with nefarious secrets and motives. Admittedly, detective fiction is populated with these perils so that, as Borges puts it, "in this chaotic era of ours" the "classic virtues" can be maintained: such stories are "safeguarding order in an era of disorder." True as this may be, is it not most frequently the case that "realistic" detection (as opposed to the "urban romance" of Chesterton's Father Brown) trades on the terrible truth that the criminal can only be caught if the soul of the detective is as corrupt as his own—a variation on evil as safeguard of goodness? Even if the good guys don't use malignant means, the genre still concentrates our attention so completely on crime and criminals that the avid reader of it (the addict, especially) might come to conclude that "life" is a mobster's paradise, and that it would be "unrealistic" to think otherwise.

Psychological realists and their stream-of-consciousness cousins not infrequently incarnate similar truths on the level of the psyche; either every apparently good aspiration is mingled with self-serving machinations, or—at best—what moves characters is, has been, and always will be woefully ambiguous and anxiously unknowable. Dostoevsky has called his own form of psychological realism "higher" because "I portray all the depths of the human soul." In part he was distancing himself from the great Balzac, whose realism required pages and pages devoted to describing the furniture his characters sat on with verisimilitude. External physical realities, Dostoevsky alleges, are less real than the soul. But what, in the soul, is *most real?* His fiction has a proclivity to concentrate our eyes on the darkness of those depths: the refined revolutionary Stavrogin and suicidal Kirilov of *Demons*; *Crime and Punishment's* Raskolnikov with his murderous resentment masked in noble motives; "The Dream of a Ridiculous Man" who corrupts the innocent inhabitants of a distant planet, to name a few. True, *Brothers Karamazov* contains the prospect of sanctity, even as it professes our proclivity toward depravity. Dmitri may confess that the "cruel insect had already grown strong in my soul," accentuating the fact that he is "filled with low desires," but Alyosha (an acolyte of holiness if there is one in their family) blushes at his brother's admissions because "The ladder's the same. I'm at the bottom step, and you're above, somewhere about the thirteenth. That's how I see it. But it's all the same. Absolutely the same in kind. Anyone on the bottom step is bound to go up to the top one." Whenever I have taught Dostoevsky a contingent of students will chide the novels for being so fantastical and unreal; "People don't act or think like this," they say. After class, as if sheepish to say so, others who have known broken families and hard times have been at the point of tears: the realist in a higher sense has read their souls.

Realism's tacit-or-telltale insistence that reality is more convoluted and chaotic and corrupt than we would wish to imagine seems, at first glance, to be a welcome imitation of our inevitable concupiscence. Even the romantic comedic Jane Austen, that inheritor of a kind of Christian Aristotelian account of the virtues, populates her novels with far more surrogates than genuine articles of goodness. As Alasdair

MacIntrye has it, she is "preoccupied in a quite new way with counterfeits of the virtues"—those who equate *being virtuous* with appearing to be so. This concern with virtue is married to a kind of nascent realism in that she "sees the telos of human life implicit in its everyday form." But if Austen had the stirrings of realism in her bones (everyday mundanity is her territory; unhappy marriages far outweigh happy ones when the fates of her novelistic corpus are tallied), many deny her admission into the realist school, citing the sense of unreality her novels incubate on account of their lack of physical description and detail. Whereas Alastair Duckworth contends that Austen subscribed to the realist dictum that "that the novelist should describe things that are really there, that imagination should be limited to an existing order," even as she enunciates that what is most "really there" are the psychological states of her characters and the social consequences of the same. Marilyn Butler, on the other hand, forbids Austen the realist badge because the novelist so strongly disapproved of "the sensuous, the irrational, [and] the involuntary types of mental experience" that, "although she cannot deny their existence, she disapproves of them." Given the aforementioned unhappy fates of so many Austen characters, it is hard to wholeheartedly concede this point; she may not imitate the darker depths familiar to Dostoevsky (Elizabeth Bennet could never have a brother like Raskolnikov), but she plays out the sad *consequences* of these irrationalities via plot and action.

Being a novelist, Flannery O'Connor contends, is synonymous with being "hotly in pursuit of the real," although the "realism of each novelist will depend on his view of the ultimate reaches of reality." In her well-known formulation, it is the "realist of distances" who is most prophetic, most profound, for she moves away from mere social patterns and dead conventions of what constitutes reality and reaches "toward mystery and the unexpected." Prophecy, she clarifies, "is a matter of seeing near things with their extensions of meaning and thus of seeing far things close up"—a phenomenon we find in the "best modern instances of the grotesque." Here again what is most real is associated with something "generally described in a pejorative sense," as something gross or defiant of propriety. But in the good grotesque of the realist of distances "we find that the writer has made alive some experience which we are not accustomed to observe every day, or which the ordinary man may never experience in his ordinary life." By necessity, then, this sort of realism will be "wild," "violent and comic" because it combines discrepancies, keen to hit on "one image that will connect or combine or embody two points; one is a point in the concrete, and the other is a point not visible to the naked eye, but believed in by him firmly, just as real to him, really, as the one that everybody sees." Not all moral vision is *moralism*. Not all spiritual vision is oversimplified false piety. An artistic vision that is richly moral and daringly prophetic, far from being unreal, picks up on the registers of actuality that pack the most being.

Crucially, for all his fidelity to mundane realities, the climax of Flaubert's *Madame Bovary* is structured around one such grotesque image—a concrete exaggeration gesturing toward an unseen point—an awful assertion of the weight of our disfigurement amidst so many romantic efforts to overcome it. Living lyrically through her litany of affairs, Emma inconveniently encounters a beggar on her way back to her blasé home:

> His shoulders were covered by a mass of rags, and a battered old beaver hat, rounded into the shape of a basin, hid his face; but when he took it off he revealed two bloody, gaping sockets in place of eyelids. The flesh was

falling away in crimson shreds, and from it oozed liquids which hardened into green scabs down to the nose, whose black nostrils were always sniffling convulsively.

Seeing this deformed man in all of his hideousness (Flaubert does not fail to force us to face it), Emma's soul is sent "into the depths of her soul, like a whirlwind in an abyss." How can she continue to assert romance in a world weighed down by such proximate, paroxysmal suffering? The two pillars of realism—"taking things as they are" and fidelity to serious imitation of everyday life—teeter when Flaubert begins to employ the beggar in a patterned manner, introducing the "ugliness of reality" at clearly-choreographed plot points. H.G. Wells rejected the fiction of Henry James on the grounds that it was too patterned; as E.M. Forster reports, Wells insisted that "life should be given the preference, and must not be whittled or distended for a pattern's sake"; if this equivocation of real life and patternlessness were accurate, any narrative form whatsoever would be forced, feigned failure. As MacIntyre points out, this was the position of Sartre: not merely that "narrative is very different from life," but that "to present human life in the form of a narrative is always to falsify it. There are not and there cannot be any true stories." Discrete actions leading nowhere, out of order and of dubious causality comprise real life, and the falsifying storyteller imposes a pattern and logic retrospectively, arbitrarily. Does Flaubert's realism fail, then, when he has the beggar show up—all too conveniently—at Emma's death bed? She has just poisoned herself and found that the death throes are far more awful than she had imagined they would be. She presses her lips to the crucified God-Man, imprinting on the cross, "with all her fading strength, the most ardent kiss of love she had ever given." Hearing her death rattle, the priest begins to accelerate his prayers, and "at times everything seemed to fade into the steady murmur of Latin syllables as they rolled on like the tolling of a bell." At this precise moment, when the lyrical again threaten to override the "real" as Flaubert conceives it, the beggar "suddenly" appears outside Emma's chambers. His heavy wooden shoes and scraping stick hint at his presence, and then his "raucous voice" leaves no doubt. The beggar arrives bearing a romantic ballad of a "young girl in an amorous way," and Emma, hearing it, "sat up like a galvanized corpse." Recognizing the blind man, she begins to laugh a "horrible, frenzied, desperate laugh, imagining that she could see the wretched beggar's hideous features looming in the shadows of eternity like the face of terror itself."

Flaubert fulfills the grotesque realism of distances Flannery O'Connor formulates, finding an image with one point in the concrete and the other invisible to the naked eye; but whereas her grotesque frequently pierces her characters with presentiments of paradise (graces they are often unwilling to readily receive), Flaubert's palpable detail has its parallel in the terrors of hell. Shadows, ugliness, hideous horrors are, as it were, *the really real.* As Victor H. Brombert reminds us, Flaubert's famous aspiration to render things dispassionately, "as God sees them" is further explained as being a representation of the "futility of subjective justification," for (says Flaubert) God's loftier perspective is synonymous with "the point of view of a superior joke."

Realism, then, as Flaubert fleshes it out, is demoralization. His demand for a new style which would be "as rhythmical as poetry, as precise as the language of the sciences, and would have undulations, the mellow throb of the cello, plumes of fire" could be a stand in for the kind of contemplative realism I am trying to advocate. His devotion to self-abnegation is admirable: "I love my work," he wrote at age thirty, "with the passionate and perverted love of an ascetic who loves the hairshirt which scratches his belly." What Harry Levin calls the "suppression of his own personality"—purportedly the premise of *Bovary*—in favor of achieving an "eloquent banality" of the everyday is an admirable aim. "I was ridden by the cancer of lyricism," he confessed to Maxime Du Camp, "and you operated; it was just in time, but I cried out in pain." As Levin observes, in *Madame Bovary* "the rhetoric is constantly expanding into purple passages which are trenchantly deflated by his irony." The uptake? Central to Flaubert's creed of "naked truth" is not just his assertion that beauty, like a star, "cannot be detached from heaven," but that reality is fundamentally an unbeautiful urge toward nonbeing. Here he confirms Virginia Woolf's sense, in "The Narrow Bridge of Art," that "there trips along by the side of our modern beauty some mocking spirit which sneers at beauty for being beautiful; which turns the looking-glass and shows us that the other side of her cheek is pitted and deformed."

Nonetheless, the theory of materialist objectivist realism as found in Flaubert's letters is repeatedly (and blessedly) interrupted in practice. As Katy Carl puts it, "his theory brackets the 'unseen,' but his novel makes it everywhere palpable." In *Madame Bovary,* the smallest creature can convey the strongest stirrings of the spirit, as when Emma Bovary's "thoughts constantly returned to that house, like the pigeons from the Lion d'Or which alighted on it to wet their pink feet and white wings in the rain gutters." Notice the *thisness* of those pink feet and white wings set in motion—wetting their bodies the way Emma's soul whets its appetite by alighting on the self-same house.

O'Connor's realism, with its "large and startling figures," is a crucial contribution to the health of the species; her stories restore our sense that the spiritual is superior to the literal, necessary and good though the latter is. Unlike Flaubert's blind-guide grotesque, her employments of the device remind us of God's power and providence. They purify us of any Manicheism which would see the created world as evil or innately wretched or would violently separate matter and spirit.

A contemplative realism, however, does not require shouts and startles; it need not distance itself from these tactics, but its habitual disposition would, if fully incarnate, combine the small child's awe with the seasoned seeing of a blind old monk who has been through it all. In *The Journey of the Mind to God*, St. Bonaventure maps an ascending ladder which would lead us from the lowest lairs of (yet beautiful) creation to the glory of God, for He has left vestiges of Himself in the visible world. Whoever is not enlightened by such great splendor in created things is blind," says Bonaventure, boldly: "whoever remains unheedful of such great outcries is deaf; whoever does not praise God in all these effects is dumb; whoever does not turn to the First Principle after so many signs is a fool." God's goodness can unfailingly be found by one who opens his eyes, alerts the ears of his spirit, applies his hearts, and opens his lips in magnification of our Maker. Far from being a conventual escapist, the contemplative is one who "considers the actual existence of things."

The actual Benedictine is the Benedictine of the actual. On the one hand, like Chesterton's Father Brown, he is well acquainted with the shadows of human hearts, as "a man who does next to nothing but hear men's real sins is not likely to be wholly unaware of human evil." On the other, he does not allow exposure to the inner recesses of wickedness to ruin his vision of all the goodness God has created. O'Connor knew that a real writer must become a contemplative: "The writer should never be ashamed of staring. There is nothing that does not require his attention." But in feeding the fruits of this true contemplation through the exaggerations of the grotesque, she affiliated the fullness of truth with a kind of wildness, a kind of dramatic desperation to reach those souls deaf and blind to God. The contemplative realist does not, primarily, resort to "shock tactics." He is primarily concerned with co-creating a prose that can heal our dulled and disenchanted vision; never hesitating to narrate human rebellion, he never loses sight of that concomitant need to cultivate and restore a vision of grandeur.

Tolkien's depiction of fantasy gives the contemplative realist much to chew on concerning the cleansing of our vision. He takes to task this tacit (and sometimes touted) assumption that "reality" is dreary. He cites a clerk of Oxenford who warmly welcomed the nearby robot factories spawning mass production nearby, for these and the "roar of self-obstructive mechanical traffic" purportedly "brought his university into 'contact with real life.'" It is flatly erroneous, Tolkien counters, to assume that "motor-cars are more 'alive' than, say, centaurs or dragons." *Sed contra*, "that they are more 'real' than, say, horses, is pathetically absurd. How startlingly alive is a factory chimney compared with an elm tree: poor obsolete thing, insubstantial dream of an escapist!" The narrowing of "reality" to ugly urbanization and to artificial advancements would require us to conclude that "the roof of Bletchley station" is more inspiring and worthy of wonder than "the legendary dome of heaven." If we translate these errors into "'serious literature'" says Tolkien, what counts as real will primarily consist of "no more than play under a glass roof by the side of a municipal swimming bath." Tolkien grants that the famed foulness represented by the realists *is* true, but, citing Christopher Dawson, he blames not the created world as it was and is (if you look long enough) and will be, but rather the "rawness and ugliness of modern European life" which is "an insufficient or false reaction to environment."

It is no accident that the novels of Alice Thomas Ellis, so often set in the gloriously jagged and sublimely remote Welsh islands, skim freely from the natural beauty surrounding in abundance to the fantastical-mythical past. As Mary sits watching her cat in *The Birds of the Air*, her gaze extends beyond the hollow, past the ridge, where the "old wolf-colored woods, grizzled with snow" remained "ground untouched by man, who could find no use for it." Now, though, "neat and placid chimneys" replaced the prehistorical forest "where the Great Worm lay curled in the declivity" beside the "saurian Cathedral, the Creator's tribute to himself before he thought of making men to praise his genius."

Fantasy, Tolkien argues, far from being an escapist illusion, restores to us a "clear view." It is not, he cautions, a claim to be "seeing things as they are" by which he would "involve [himself] with the philosophers," but rather "seeing things as we are (or were) meant to see them—as things apart from ourselves." Far more than underlying ugliness, the self-reinforcing effects of drab triteness and familiarity constitute our problem. In turn these obfuscating attitudes are the "penalty of 'appropriation,'" the "legal or mental" assumption of possession, for though beautiful things are real and have a full share of being, once we "acquired" them we "ceased to look at them."

While an adherence to the *realist* side of contemplative realism forbids outright fantasy as a corrective to the alliance of "the real" with disenchanted, naked, and often violent truth, he nonetheless strives for something of the same end as at least one of the aims of his fiction. In Joseph Conrad's words, he "appeals to that part of our being" which is "a gift and not an acquisition."

The contemplative realist, considering the actual existence of things, at once sees them as we were meant to see them and also shows the rest of us how to see them. Sometimes he shows us the same thing several times, in several ways, leading us up the ladder of perception to a fuller share in the beauty of being: superficially first, operating in the mode of "how things are" in their apparent blasé "nothing to see here" state, or scattered in apparent disorder; then, as St. Bonaventure puts it, "he considers things in themselves," namely, in their matter and substance, power and activity, measure and motion, and from here "the observer can rise, as from a vestige, to the knowledge of the immense power, wisdom, and goodness of the Creator." The contemplative, as contemplative, can achieve this ascent without needing to communicate it at all. No one, says Bonaventure, "arrives at contemplation except through penetrating meditation, holy living, and devout prayer." The contemplative realist surely needs these things and more. Wedded to the word and world in a different manner, the contemplative realist must manifest this perception in his prose.

There is something of the Russian formalist Viktor Shklovsky's "*enstrangement*" in his modus operandi. He agrees with Shklovsky that one purpose of art is to "lead us to a knowledge of a thing through the organ of sight instead of recognition. By 'enstranging' objects and complicating form, the device of art makes perception long and 'laborious.' The perceptual process in art has a purpose all its own and ought to be extended to the fullest." With the enstranger he describes a thing "as if it were perceived for the first time, while an incident is described as if it were happening for the first time." Showing the reader how to stare rightly, he does more than merely make things goodly weird. Yes, he relishes what Hopkins calls "all things counter, original, spare, and strange," but he delights in one oddness above all else—Bonaventure's notion that "creatures are shadows, echoes, and pictures of that first, most powerful, most wise and most perfect Principle, of that first eternal Source, Light, Fullness, of that first efficient and exemplary and ordering Art." Creatures are "exemplars, or rather illustrations offered to souls as yet untrained, and immersed in the senses, so that through sensible things that they see they may be transported to the intelligible which they do not see." Given this, he discerns and demonstrates the hierarchies in existence, registering that which is "changeable and corruptible" is inferior to that which is "changeless and incorruptible," inculcating in us a way of weighing what is passing *sub specie aeternitatis*.

St. Ignatius embodies something of this mode when, in the *Exercises*, he advises the retreatant to begin his or her contemplation of the Annunciation to Mary by beginning quite far from her humble pinpoint spot: "the first point is to see the persons on either side: first, those on the face of the earth so varied in dress and carriage; some white and others black; some in peace and others war; some weeping, others laughing; some in health, others sick; some being born, others dying." Then, with a similarly grand grasp after the globe, the retreatant should "hear what people are saying on the face of the earth; how they converse together, how they blaspheme . . . likewise what the Three Divine Persons are saying . . . and then what the angel and Our Lady are saying." We can only aspire to hear what God is saying by beginning with the earthly inhabitants' exhilarations and agonies, their whispers and shouts. Amidst this din the Trinity speaks. What does God say to our characters as they sing and strive and sin?"

Being a realist, the devotee of contemplative realism is keenly cognizant of concupiscence. Sometimes a character can only behold the beautiful in a manner that ushers melancholy, as when, in Woolf's *Jacob's Room*, several souls are staring into the sky; "Doesn't it make you melancholy—looking at the stars?" one woman asks, channeling Pascal's petrified terror in the presence of infinite spaces.

Other times the beautiful is juxtaposed with pain and strain. When the contemplative realist becomes more painterly, pausing to overtly notice details, he slows down the story's action, arresting and cultivating the attention of the reader even amidst climactic conflict. Willa Cather is one of the novelist painters *par excellence*. She remarked that "I think 'Two Friends' is the best short story I have ever done. It's a little like a picture by Courbet; has that queer romantic sort of realism."

Just before the most consequential moment in her story "Two Friends," Willa Cather pulls out the paintbrush and applies the acrylic liberally, going so far as to employ the painting metaphor as she places us in a run-down section of the city: "These abandoned buildings, an eyesore by day, melted together into a curious pile in the moonlight, became an immaterial structure of velvet-white and glossy blackness, with here and there a faint smear of blue door, or a tilted patch of sage-green that had once been a shutter."

In contrast to these decrepit buildings and environs made glorious by the narrator's brushing eye (her description is more extensive than the passage I just cited), the scene switches to an event that is intrinsically awesome, but which receives less tangibles: "Then we saw a bright wart on the other edge of the moon, but for a second only, — the machinery up there worked fast. While the two men were exclaiming and telling me to look, the planet swung clear of the golden disk, a rift of blue came between them and widened very fast. The planet did not seem to move, but that inky blue space between it and the moon seemed to spread. The thing was over."

Here it is an act of aesthetic justice that the transit of Venus receives only a few quick if clarifying sensuous strokes—that is, it performs a correct mimesis of the narrator's memory, because the narrator remembers the event as happening very fast. Additionally, the diction Cather applies implies the story's underlying truth: lacking a true foundation, the friendship of the "Two Friends" is imperiled. There is a "wart" on the illumining moon. A "rift of blue" comes between these heavenly bodies, even as one character's political commitments will imminently rend what remains of their relationship.

"Let me see," Mr. Trueman remarked slowly, "they reckon the moon's about two hundred and fifty thousand miles away from us. I wonder how far that star is."

"I don't know, J. H., and I really don't much care. When we can get the tramps off the railroad, and manage to run this town with one fancy house instead of two, and have a Federal Government that is as honest as a good banking business, then it will be plenty of time to turn our attention to the stars."

Here we have it—that "queer romantic sort of realism," something very close to a contemplative realism. Mr. Trueman and Mr. Dillon have sustained friendly conversations in spite of political divergences. Dillon's political realism results in a repudiation of contemplative realism: he can only scoff at Trueman's infectious wonder, a wonder Cather cultivates extensively through her own prose, which so masterfully pauses and draws out both the beauty and what mars it. The wonder doesn't lead Trueman to God, but he is close to the truth. Dillon's concern for the country is noble, but political commitment ought not to necessitate suspension of the cosmos' significance.

In his germ of natural theology in *Romans*, St. Paul says

that the truth about creation has been suppressed because men failed to honor or thank God. Ungrateful, bereft of reverence, their capacity to see vestiges of Him in creation became blunted:

> For what can be known about God is plain to them, because God has shown it to them. Ever since the creation of the world his eternal power and divine nature, invisible though they are, have been understood and seen through the things he has made. So they are without excuse; for though they knew God, they did not honor him as God or give thanks to him, but they became futile in their thinking, and their senseless minds were darkened (Romans 1:19-21).

If we are to perceive God in creation, then we need to cultivate gratitude and honor or we too will miss the marks and, in turn, miss the Maker.

The poet and fictionist (and capable contemplative realist) Seth Wieck has developed this point: the two contrary dispositions—ingratitude vs. gratitude—find counterpoints in parallel scenes of Cormac McCarthy's *Blood Meridian* and Marilynne Robinson's *Gilead.*

In *Blood Meridian*, McCarthy moves us into a makeshift cemetery filled with the graves of men who fell in battle. The slabs are unmarked. As the men witness two points of light in the distance the narrator concludes that "if there are worlds burning past the two poles, then they are beyond our knowing." Nature, for the narrator, is *not clear enough*, but we can't help but wonder if his own mind is unduly darkened. The spiritual spinout of that darkness is evident in yet another passage painting the desert sun:

> In the neuter austerity of that terrain all phenomena were
> bequeathed a strange equality and no one thing nor spider
> nor stone nor blade of grass could put forth claim to pre-
> cedence . . . [I]n the optical democracy of such landscapes
> all preference is made whimsical and a man and a rock
> become endowed with unguessed kinships.

As Wieck demonstrates, Robinson provides a coun-
terpoint to this scene in *Gilead*. A father and son sit in an
abandoned cemetery. A rising moon overtakes the setting
sun. Robinson trains our attention on the luminous charge
pouring through the points of light, points that reach the son
and his father. The boy kisses the father's hand as he prays,
and the father, not ignorant of the death marks around them,
says "I'm grateful to know that there can be beauty in a place
like this."

The contemplative realist is also trained to register the
separate parts of creation as bearing different levels of significance depending on the story's situation. Not every description or detail needs to ascend from the sensuous literal to
mystical union with God. To assert so would be to forge a
sort of forced, inhuman transcendence. Not everything needs
to irradiate with the same significance. And yet, at times,
something quite mundane (the acceptance of the ordinary
and mundanity is key for contemplative realists) is actively
perceived in a manner that draws us into the depths of our
nature. Woolf does this wonderfully, again in *Jacob's Room*:

> Let us consider letters—how they come at breakfast, and
> at night, with their yellow stamps and their green stamps,
> immortalized by the postmark—for to see one's own enve-
> lope on another's table is to realize how soon deeds sever
> and become alien. Then at last the power of the mind to

quit the body is manifest, and perhaps we fear or hate or wish annihilated this phantom of ourselves, lying on the table. Still, there are letters that merely say how dinner's at seven; others ordering coal; making appointments. The hand in them is scarcely perceptible, let alone the voice or the scowl. Ah, but when the post knocks and the letter comes always the miracle seems repeated—speech attempted. Venerable are letters, infinitely brave, forlorn, and lost.

How fully Woolf fulfills Conrad's call to "snatch, in a moment of courage, from the remorseless rush of time a passing phase of life" and then, in "tenderness and faith" to "hold up unquestioningly" the "rescued fragment before all eyes in the light of a sincere mood" through which its "movement, its form, and its color, reveal the substance of its truth—disclose its inspiring secret." If he achieves her difficult good, the contemplative realist will (again Conrad) "awaken in the hearts of the beholders that feeling of unavoidable solidarity; of the solidarity in mysterious origin, in toil, in joy, in hope, in uncertain fate, which binds men to each other and all mankind to the visible world."

To be sure he reads rightly that which he sees with his eyes which witness things so intensely—to be sure he doesn't distort and warp reality—the practitioner of contemplative realism must, in the exclusive sense, *become* a Christian contemplative. The ideal source and summit to the formation of his soul and sensibility would be the liturgy, that pinnacle of holiness and beauty. And there is no need for a false dichotomy: the ascent of his soul to the altar of God in no way, realist that he is, leaves him less attentive to the world as it is; he knows the singular woes which afflict his age and strives to spy the practical possibilities for good. Being a gleaner of the choicest words, He must contemplate Christ in the Word of God and all of the manifestation of God's grace from Genesis to Apocalypse. Maybe especially significant, for the literary artist, are the Psalms with their (*De Profundis*) range of human dispositions toward God. More: he should spend significant time meditating upon God's attributes, His perfections of simplicity and infinity, immensity and eternity, His being and his goodness. Given the gravity that can keep us too self-bound, how good it is to dwell on that greatest good—God—"that than which nothing greater can be thought." Fictionists are inevitably recorders of defects, but how can we register the extent of defection without comparison to the perfection of Being? As St. Bonaventure asks, "How could the intellect know that a specific being is defective and incomplete if it had no knowledge of the Being that is free from all defect?" as "privations and defects can in no way be known except through something positive."

Contemplative realists need more than even this capacity to compare privations and imperfections with Perfection Incarnate. Human *phronesis*, practical wisdom, may yet pause at the crucial moment that calls for decisiveness. "Even infused prudence," advises Father Garrigou-Lagrange, "hesitates, for example" discursively weighing "what answer to give to an indiscreet question so as to avoid a lie and keep a secret; while a special inspiration of the Holy Ghost will enable us to find a proper [superdiscursive] reply, as Christ told His disciples." Writing knotted scenes of privations, paining over the problems of morality and literature, striving to imitate the mysterious intersection of beatific grace and many-faced nature, whispering or shouting God's own glories—no contemplative realist approaching these difficulties can complete the demands of both art and faith by means of prudence alone. Solely the Holy Ghost can do that. Only he can give sufficient gifts at the artist's dire hour of room-pacing, red-eyed, head-scratching need.

He can join St. Bonaventure in his mystical-philosophical journey of the mind toward God, moving from the presence of God in his visible vestiges to His image imprinted on our natural powers, finding that "memory is an image of eternity" and interiorizing the primacy of the Good for all human desires: "So great is the power of the highest Good that nothing can be loved by a creature except through the desire for that Good, so that he who takes the likeness and the copy for truth errs and goes astray." Contemplative realists capture characters' misguidance as resultant from a false identification of the good. Their stories are ridden with arcs tracing the characters' painful epiphanies when they recognize that the apparent goods they had pursued with such ardor are actually causes of their own undoing. These writers also recognize the treasury of dramatic tension found in situations where a single character must choose not between good and evil but among competing goods. Still more, they portray genuine goods *as goods*, not as innate evils, even when characters pursue the wrong goods at the wrong times with the wrong people.

Entrance into His image can also be overwhelming, because the discrepancy between Divine perfection and human frailty is overwhelming. As St. Teresa of Avila counsels, "Still, we should remember that the bee is constantly flying about from flower to flower, and in the same way, believe me, the soul must sometimes emerge from self-knowledge and soar aloft in meditation upon the greatness and the majesty of its God. Doing this will help it to realize its own baseness better than thinking of its own nature, and it will be freer from the reptiles which enter the first rooms—that is, the rooms of self-knowledge." In short, "we shall never succeed in knowing ourselves unless we seek to know God." Nonetheless, though, "We get a distorted idea of our own nature, and, if we never stop thinking about ourselves," she insists that "self-knowledge is so important that, even if you were raised right up to the heavens, I should like you never to relax your cultivation of it; so long as we are on this earth, nothing matters more to us than humility." While, even over centuries, few writers will match the abnegation of the saints, we can alternately marvel over them in shock and befuddlement and emulate their realism as far as we are able. As Francois Mauriac admits in *God and Mammon,* the saints, with their manifestations of humility, seemed perverse in documenting their shortcomings given their poise at the "height of perfection." Later, however, he submitted to the sense that "As the saints advance in the double knowledge of God and of their own souls, they get such a piercing vision of their unworthiness that they abase themselves and annihilate themselves by the most natural of instincts." It is "precisely their sanctity that makes them see [their corruptions] so lucidly." This sanctified realism is one of the rarest and most astonishing peaks of self-knowledge.

Only by emulating this impossible miracle will the contemplative realist be able to fully embody Mauriac's conclusion that "if there is a reason for the novelist on earth it is this: to show the element which holds out against God in the highest and noblest characters—the innermost evils and dissimulations; and also to light up the secret source of sanctity in creatures who seem to us to have failed."

From His image "purified, enlightened, and perfected in us through gifts of grace we can pass to considerations of the Divine Unity and Most Blessed Trinity in being and goodness. The mind, like Martha, is "distracted by many cares," Bonaventure warns, and therefore fails to recognize "God's closeness to our souls." We are drawn elsewhere by concupiscence and "beclouded by sense images." Fallen, the only way we can "enter into [ourselves] to delight in the Lord except through the mediation of Christ." Remember that even this entrance into God's image in ourselves remains just that, an image, "and this indeed is to *see through a mirror in an obscure manner.*"

Finally, with pseudo-Dionysius he should ask for that spiritual and mystical transport of the mind in which our restless understanding receives rest and God alone receives our affections:

> Abandon the senses, intellectual activities, and all visible and invisible things—everything that is not and everything that is—and, oblivious of yourself, let yourself be brought back, in so far as it is possible, to union with Him who is above all essence and all knowledge. And transcending yourself and all things, ascend to the superessential gleam of the divine darkness by an incommensurable and absolute transport of a pure mind.

Too hard a task, you say? Superhuman, even. Yes! As Father James V. Schall, SJ explains, "contemplative life is not properly human but superhuman. St. Thomas even says that *homo naturaliter non est humanus sed superhumanus est*, so that things that are human point to what is beyond human nature." Humanly speaking, we cannot catch a glimpse of that superessential gleam. But, St. Bonaventure counsels, we can "die and enter into this darkness" insofar as we "silence all our cares, our desires, and our imaginings," and submit to the "Bridegroom, not the teacher," to the "fire that wholly inflames and carries one into God through transporting unctions and consuming affections."

Nonetheless, O'Connor's perception must ground us, restoring our contemplative aims: "we are made out of dust, and if you scorn getting yourself dusty, then you shouldn't try to write fiction. It's not a grand enough job for you."

The patron of contemplative realism must be St. Teresa of Avila, renowned for her assurance that "God moves amidst the pots and pans." The practical mystic had no place for highfalutin ascetical aspirants who, attempting to leave mundanity for the heights of "union with God," thereby failed to do small things with great love. Nothing was too miniscule for St. Teresa's soul. "In all the things that have been created by so great and wise a God there must be many secrets by which we can profit," she professed, offering a crucial qualification: "although I believe that in every little thing created by God there is more than we realize, even in so small a thing as a tiny ant."

Regular realists also treasure ants. Consider this passage from Stephen Crane's *Red Badge of Courage* depicting a dead soldier's decaying corpse: "The mouth was open. Its red had changed to an appalling yellow. Over the gray skin of the face ran little ants. One was trundling some sort of a bundle along the upper lip." As James Wood remarks of this passage, the ants are "busily indifferent to human activity." The ants are imitated not so much to probe their mystery but more so to record, with anti-sentimental assertion, the absurdities of existence.

Another insect—this time a fly—appears at the end of Dostoevsky's *The Idiot*, in the presence of a recently murdered main character, Nastasya Fillippovna. Here I cannot help noting, given Dostoevsky's (possibly apocryphal) declaration that "We all came of Gogol's 'Overcoat,'" the clear affinities between this scene from *The Idiot* and a remark near the end of "The Overcoat." When the protagonist Akakii Akakievich dies, Gogol observes that "a human being just disappeared and left no trace, a human being who no one ever dreamed of protecting . . . whom no one thought of taking any interest in, who did not attract the attention of even a naturalist who never fails to stick a pin through an ordinary fly to examine it under the microscope." Mulling this juxtaposition of human mortality and dissection of the microscopic fly, the contemplative realist is keenly aware of the difference between the necessarily clinical gaze of the scientist and the mesmerized smittenness of the contemplative.

Let's see how Dosty (as Kerouac called him) the realist "in a higher sense" registers the creature. "The fly," says Allen Tate, "appears out of nowhere in the last scene in *The Idiot*: out of nowhere, but only if we limit our apperception of place to the scale of the human will." Rogozhin and Myshkin—doubles from the start—stand over the dead body of Nastasya. Myshkin, "the idiot," has been in love with Nastasya from the beginning, as has Rogozhin, though the latter's "love" is more like lust whereas the former's amounts to a tormented and misguided attempt to treat her with mercy. Rogozhin can only "possess" the woman who resists him by murdering her:

> At the end of the bed there was a crumpled heap of lace and on the white lace the toes of a bare foot peeped out from under the sheet; it seemed as though it had been carved out of marble and it was horridly still. Myshkin looked and felt that as he looked the room became more still and deathlike. Suddenly there was the buzz of a fly which flew over the bed and settled on the pillow.

Tate reads the fly as standing "in its sinister and abundant life for the privation of life, the body of the young woman on the bed." In the silence, we see that any "sinister significance that the fly may create in us is entirely due to its crossing our own path. By means of the fly the human order is compromised."

It is possible that Dostoevsky's fly, more than Crane's ants, amount to nearly the same thing. But Dostoevsky's description is less ironic, less acclimated to what Wood calls Crane's "calm horror." By one word it resists any anti-sentimental celebration of life's heartless onward march: "Suddenly." That suddenness shocks us, tells us that we *should* be unsettled by the unwelcome intrusion.

Or should we? Is it really that strange that nature would "intrude" upon our indoor realm? As Carl Schmitt put it, in a world transformed beyond recognition by technology and industry, "Nature appears today as the polar antithesis of the mechanistic world of big cities, whose stone, iron, and glass structures lie on the face of the earth like colossal Cubist configurations. The antithesis of this empire of technology is nature untouched by civilization, wild and barbarian—a reservation into which 'man with his affliction does not set foot.' Such a dichotomy between a rationalistic-mechanistic world of human labor and a romantic-virginal state of nature is totally foreign to the Roman Catholic concept of nature." Be that as it may, in the limited and non-omniscient comprehension of a mortal human, the fly *is* an intrusion insofar as it desecrates the vestige of God's image found in the human being. I think of *Mouchette,* by Georges Bernanos, the raw realist and visionary. *Mouchette* is a brilliant short tragedy that concentrates almost entirely on the brutal sufferings and spiritual desperation of an abused and impoverished girl in rural France, but the last pages of the novel accentuate rare beauty espied amidst the depravity. A wise and wizened old woman appears on the scene, channeling grace through the subtlest of actions. Tender of the local dead, "no crease in the sheet could escape her vigilance. Her fleshless, long-nailed finger would stretch against the cloth as she straightened it out. No wandering fly was allowed to remain near the face which, as soon as she had taken up her watch, was covered by a white handkerchief." A sort of sacred veiling of the human face both protects the dead from indignity and asks us to keep wake, to share in what Bernanos calls the corpse-keeper's "enigmatic contemplation."

But the contemplative realist will strive to see and say still more. He will render such a scene while keeping in mind St. Augustine's counsel in *City of God*: "because we ourselves, by reason of our mortality, are so enmeshed in this corner of the cosmos that we fail to perceive the beauty of the total pattern in which the particular parts, which seem ugly to us, blend in so harmonious and beautiful a way." Regularly, "it is a case of regarding only their utility, not the things themselves . . . But with such reasoning, fault could be found even with the sun, since criminals and debtors have sometimes been judicially condemned to solar exposure." Intrinsic to nature itself are predatory creatures and prey. The existence of the former is not evil, but rather, Augustine insists, "the very law of transitory things here on earth." The same holds for the ants and the fly, although their authors do not grant us sufficient perspective and distance to see the scene with St. Augustine's realism.

Do not misunderstand me. I am not asking for a dizzying perspective that would veritably damn humanity, the sort found in Stephen Crane's incredible story "The Blue Hotel":

> We picture the world as thick with conquering and elate
> humanity, but here with the bugles of the tempest pealing
> it was hard to imagine a peopled earth. One viewed the

existence of man then as a marvel, and conceded a glamour of wonder to these lice which were caused to cling to a whirling, fire-smitten, ice-locked, disease-stricken, space-lost bulb. The conceit of man was explained by this storm to be the very engine of life.

Note the "realistic" enunciation of the decrepit and terroristic features of the natural world, and man's *affiliation* (not merely contrast) with petty lice. Waxing lyrical and hyperbolical as ever, Myles Connolly's Mr. Blue gives beautiful voice to what's remarkable, what's worth preserving in the Christian vision of man in creation: "Without Christ we would be little more than bacteria breeding on a pebble in space or glints of ideas in a whirling void of abstractions. Because of him, I can stand here out under this cold immensity and know that my infinitesimal pulse-beats and acts and thoughts are of more importance than this whole show of a universe." The contemplative realist occupies an incarnational middle ground between the fixation on Nature found in Crane and the humanism of Henry James. In "The Middle Years," James depicts the sickly Dencombe who "sat and stared at the sea, which appeared all surface and twinkle, far shallower than the spirit of man. It was the abyss of human illusion that was the real, the tideless deep." In the Great Chain of Being man *is* higher than water or lice, but the contemplative realist regularly presences the pulsating being of creation beyond our consciousness. Even if mankind at the pinnacle of creation, even if the interior souls of characters are far more unfathomable and potent than the peak of a mountain, that mountain is still worth drawing out—as are littler links on the Great Chain.

Consider not the lobster but David Foster Wallace's very short story "Incarnations of Burned Children." As Mommy and Daddy tend to the nightmare of an accidentally scalded baby who "still made fists" in a last sign of life, "a bird in the oak across the driveway appeared to observe the door with a cocked head as the cries still came from inside." This "lark on the limb with its head to the side" is simultaneously as if an image of heightened concern and a being who transcends the terror of this house of pain, perched above it all just as the boy's spirit will soon be also, when

> the child had learned to leave himself and watch the whole rest unfold from a point overhead, and whatever was lost never thenceforth mattered, and the child's body expanded and walked about and drew pay and lived its life untenanted, a thing among things, it's self's soul so much vapor aloft, falling as rain and then rising, the sun up and down like a yoyo.

Here as in so many places Wallace combines the consequential and the picayune—the spirit and the plaything: no yoyo is too small to signify the soul.

And no grasshopper is too small to signify the persistence of creation's goodness over against the depths of tragic losses and traumatic events. In Katy Carl's novel *As Earth Without Water*, as a central character attempts to look away from his own significant wounds long enough to show newfound kindness to another person, the fabled insect mutely speaks of the manner in which their past connection has spent itself on momentary pleasure without storing anything up for the oncoming winter in which all three creatures now shiver. The grasshopper's "filigree wings pulse against its small body. Its chitinous legs scrabble. It hops in an ellipse atop the granite like a person looking for a lost possession." This creaturely vividness, like that of Wallace's lark, instances at once the subrational creation's relation to and unconcern with the human drama unfolding in its presence.

The constrictions of a "manifesto" forbid full development of another direction the contemplative realist would do well to plumb: the interpenetration of nature and man in such manmade things as music and architecture, both of which emerge as presences whose meanings and moods alter the actions of human beings. Take *The Strudlhof Steps* by the Catholic convert Heimito von Doderer, wherein the famous Viennese staircase becomes an indispensable force—a thing shaped by the human heart and mind which, in turn, affects the hearts and minds of those who ascend and descend, against its "lighted gateway like a gold background—the steps, the Strudlhof Steps, the stage of life ready for a dramatic performance." In Doderer's hands, the stairs become more than a mere stage; at times they influence action. As Dietrich von Hildebrand argues in his *Aesthetics*, architecture is unique in its combination of outer and inner realities. In Doderer's novel, one character revisits his favorite haunt in search of a "spatial homing place[], a geometrical space in which inner and outer topography coincided, one could say, each gaining thereby in concreteness and luminosity." The raw, unmediated being of creation, then, comprises only part of the drama. Jacques Maritain provokes this point in *Creative Intuition in Art and Poetry*: "The bay of Rio de Janeiro, immense, luminous, exquisitely delineated, is one of the most rightly admired natural sites. But how much more beautiful, how much more moving—I mean moving the very sense of beauty—is the entrance, at nightfall, into the port of Marseilles, as it opens its man-managed secretive basins one after another, in a forest of masts, cranes, lights, and memories!" Correcting undue accent on the exquisite and the elegant, the realist in us insists on representing the other (rubbed-off, faceless) side of the coin: the way the inharmonious shapes of squalor and ugly tenements, hideous high-rises and gaudy kitsch, warp or war with the human soul.

Contemplative realism remains committed to the gains that came from the realist's insistence that everyday life possesses true dignity and consequentiality. Never far from its tongue-tied wonder is Henry James' celebration of the small and insignificant of the earth. In his preface to *The Portrait of a Lady*, he remembers "how absolutely, how inordinately, the Isabel Archers, and even much smaller female fry, insist on mattering" (his own Catherine Sloper, the unassuming heroine of *Washington Square*, comes to mind). George Eliot has admirably noted it—"In these frail vessels is borne onward through the ages the treasure of human affection." The contemplative realist is ever alert to forgotten souls who "insist on mattering." She goes further, insisting that mundane decisions have eternal significance; each infinitesimal yes or no of our days tips the divine scales closer to salvation or damnation. It never forgets that the first serious treatment of everyday life was found not in Flaubert but in the Gospels. Auerbach focuses specifically on Peter's denial scene, as it dramatizes "tremendous 'pendulation'" in the heart of a fisherman, a man whom pagan antiquity could only have treated comically. But Peter's denial as set forth in the Gospel account "is too serious for comedy, too contemporary and everyday for tragedy, politically too insignificant for history— and the form which was given it is one of such immediacy that its like does not exist." The text employs direct discourse between a maid ("And thou also was with Jesus of Nazareth!") and Peter. Auerbach draws out the radicality of the Gospel on the literary level: "The random fisherman or publican or rich youth, the random Samaritan or adulteress, come from their random everyday circumstances to be immediately confronted with the personality of Jesus; and the reaction of an individual in such a moment is necessarily a matter of profound significance." The sacred vertical not only intersects with the earthly horizontal, but does so through a Person whose grace is palpably and consequentially present in the back alleys of mundanity. Contemplative realists remember this intersection as recorded by the Gospels and render analogous encounters in our time.

It would seem that those who narrate providence are transgressing the limits of imitation: how can grace, the precise workings of which none of us can pinpoint, be *shown*? Christic imaginers would, at first glance, seem to be committing a crass immoderation, feigning a kind of "mastery of God" and His work by deciphering His workings too surely. "We may be able to grasp," says Josef Pieper, "in faith the actuality and the ultimate meaning of God's working in history. But no man can presume on his own to point to any providential happening of the here and now, and to say: 'God has manifested His intention in this or that reward or punishment, confirmation or rejection.'"

As Michael D. O'Brien clarifies, "Pieper is not for a moment implying that we should cease trying to 'read' what God is saying through the rich matrix of experience. The important point is that we are called to try to apprehend, *without presumption*, what He may be revealing to us, teaching us, shaping us." The contemplative realist, cognizant that attempts to apprehend His mysterious movements can go awry, nonetheless obeys the first word of St. Benedict's *Rule*: "Listen!"

There is a major difference between our presuming to pinpoint the providential happenings in history, or the composer of the lives of the saints specifying the workings of grace in a particular soul, and the fiction writer fitting divine things to his form. In the former case, the writer is saying what God *did*, whereas the fictionist is showing us, to paraphrase Aristotle's *Poetics*, "the kind of thing that God *would* do." Given our knowledge of God as infinite, merciful, just, perfect, what sort of intervention would *this* God make in the lives of *these* kinds of characters? Importantly, in the latter case, we are dealing with hypothetical probabilities, with plausibility, which, as James Wood says, "involves the defense of the credible *imagination* against the incredible. This is surely why Aristotle writes that a convincing impossibility in mimesis is always preferable to an unconvincing possibility." A student of mine, Angie Robb, articulates the core matter of discerning and depicting divine probabilities succinctly: "it is a participation, not a presumption."

Father Reginald Garrigou-Lagrange advises an attendant caution against presumption in his book *Reality*: "The divine judgment, which gives a special mercy to one and not to another, is inscrutable. But it would not be inscrutable if grace were given by reason of a good natural disposition, since we could answer: God gave grace to this man and not to this other, because the first did, and the second did not, prepare himself thereto by his natural powers." On the natural level, this sort of reasoning is already problematic in that God's grace has so clearly (exhibit B = me) been bestowed upon sinners who have not prepared themselves for the reception of this grace by habituation into the natural virtues. Still more, as Father Garrigou-Lagrange points out, "such explanation would destroy the mystery, would lose from sight the immeasurable distance between the two orders, one of nature, the other of grace."

In *Dei Filius*, the First Vatican Council encouraged reason's impassioned pursuits while also fostering reverence in the presence of things too great for us:

Reason illustrated by faith, when it zealously, piously, and soberly seeks, attains with the help of God some understanding of the mysteries, and that a most profitable one, not only from the analogy of those things which it knows naturally, but also from the connection of the mysteries among themselves and with the last end of man; nevertheless, it is never capable of perceiving those mysteries in the way it does the truths which constitute its own proper object. For, divine mysteries by their nature exceed the created intellect so much that, even when handed down by revelation and accepted by faith, they nevertheless remain covered by the veil of faith itself, and wrapped in a certain mist, as it were, as long as in this mortal life, "we are absent from the Lord: for we walk by faith and not by sight" [*2 Cor* 5:6 f.].

The contemplative realist seeks to *presence* this veil, to dramatize mystery's hiddenness. For instance, a character might be confident that he can subject the purportedly inscrutable to his scintillating intelligence, only to come up against the limits of the latter. In Robert Louis Stevenson's *Strange Case of Dr. Jekyll and Mr. Hyde,* the lawyer Utterson sets out to *see* the wicked Mr. Hyde, sure that once his face is brought out into the light "the mystery would lighten and perhaps roll altogether away, as was the habit of mysterious things when well examined." As he gets closer and closer to the evasive heart of darkness, Utterson could well cite the words of Flannery O'Connor, words every contemplative realist mulls every day: "evil is not simply a problem to be solved, but a mystery to be endured."

The contemplative realist remembers well O'Connor's further insistence that "life from the standpoint of the central Christian mystery" has "for all its horror, been found by God to be worth dying for." Note O'Connor's nod to the many horrors that surround us. The underbellies of our civilizations and the cesspools rank in the pockets of our souls are *real*. They rightly make us reel. Sometimes the vestiges of God in the world can seem scarce or scattered relative to the apparent success of raw evil. At this juncture the contemplative realist seeks to stoke reverence for the reality of the Paschal mystery—a passion, death and Resurrection that is more real than an infinite tally of the sins and the frightening fissures, the apparently irreversible cracks in existence. But, countenancing the same absurdities that unnerved Camus and the existentialists, the contemplative realist will prevent his story's perspective from relishing the farcical or capitulating to the cruel to the point of souring cynical even as (fiction being largely a record of man in rebellion), a large part of his work consists of drawing out the spiritual intensities of man's refusal to serve.

Georges Bernanos said of Balzac that "not a single feature is to be added to any one of those frightful characters, but he has not been down to the secret spring, to the last recess of conscience where evil organizes from within, against God and for the love of death, that part of us the harmony of which has been destroyed by original sin." Too much contemporary fiction presents actual evils in a materialist manner, failing to chill us with the gelid metaphysical breath of the hell-bound. If we need more compelling good characters, souls whose virtues are represented as hard-won, balanced as if on a thin birch branch, we also need more descendants of Dostoevsky's infernal revolutionaries. Consider Dosty's Stavrogin, "hero" of *Demons*, whom Rene Girard calls a "monstrous and satanic incarnation" of supposed success. Stavrogin's revolution is not all-too-human so much as it is supra-human: his model is Satan. In a world wherein most characters live as though

God is dead, transcendence is nonetheless inescapable; their longing for the transcendent will be directed at a man rather than a divinity, and "men will be gods for each other," even as this "deviated transcendency is a caricature of vertical transcendency," for "there is not one element of this distorted mysticism which does not have its luminous counterpart in Christian truth." Characters kneel before Stavrogin. His wickedness conjures up stuttering sycophants whose enslavement far surpasses the this-worldly noddings of mere political yes men. True, the luciferian grotesquery of Stavrogin's success—his handsome, winsome mastery over so many slavish disciples—might be alleged as "unreal" by some conventional realists. But Dostoevsky's realism cannot rest with the merely material; such would be to deny an entire vista of existence. As Girard explains, Dostoevsky reveals to us that "the passion that drives men to seize or gain possession is not materialistic," but rather "the triumph of the mediator, the god with the human face."

I do not mean to indicate that the contemplative realist reads *all* human action as superhuman. The contemplative realist does not dispense with the category of nature. The great Catholic poet Dante Alighieri advanced our application of a "four-fold method" or "allegory of the theologians," which he famously outlines in a letter to his patron and protector Cangrande I, Lord of Verona. Dante explains how his work ought to be read; it is not *merely* spiritual or *merely* literal:

> rather, it may be called "polysemous," that is, of many senses. A first sense derives from the letters themselves, and a second from the things signified by the letters. We call the first sense "literal" sense, the second the "allegorical," or "moral" or "anagogical." To clarify this method of treatment, consider this verse: *When Israel went out of Egypt,*

the house of Jacob from a barbarous people: Judaea was made his sanctuary, Israel his dominion [Psalm 113]. Now if we examine the letters alone, the exodus of the children of Israel from Egypt in the time of Moses is signified; in the allegory, our redemption accomplished through Christ; in the moral sense, the conversion of the soul from the grief and misery of sin to the state of grace; in the anagogical sense, the exodus of the holy soul from slavery of this corruption to the freedom of eternal glory . . . they can all be called allegorical.

This interpretive framework, inherited from medieval biblical exegesis, trains the mind to see a given literary work as *saturated* with meanings—literal, allegorical, moral, and anagogical. As Umberto Eco jocularly remarks, here Dante "tak[es] a way of reading the bible as an example of how to read his own mundane poem!" The joke has a consequential uptake: unlike Sacred Scripture, human fictions are not saturated with meaning. The contemplative realist carefully and cautiously aspires to imbue his "mundane" or non-sacred literature with a mystical sense; in part he does this to elicit wonder, a humbling of ourselves before Mystery. To try and charge every single literal particular with an aura of transcendence would be to undertake a rivalry with God. True, literal scenes in the Scriptures are historically real in themselves but lead onward in harmony through the other levels of meaning toward the utmost Real, which is the interaction of God and man in salvation history and, finally, the union of the soul with God in paradise.

There is no contradiction between these levels of exegesis; the tangible literal, for the contemplative realist, is in harmony with the suggested spiritual. A naturalistic literature is in error insofar as it portrays the literal as all there is—as if the moral and the spiritual are wishful superimpositions. Novelist and artist Michael O'Brien raises another crucial clarification: "literal depiction in [much] modern literature, for example, does not give us the Real; a most obvious example of which is a blatantly pornographic scene claiming to be realism while in actuality destroying the real nature of the characters." The contemplative realist recognizes the beauty of directness in truth-telling but does not confuse scenes that reveal character with scenes that obscure and exploit it—and excessively exhibitive depiction of human sexuality cannot help but do the latter.

In all matters, the contemplative realist is constantly discerning which rung of the ladder a given scene or even a given sentence seeks to represent. He is ever calibrating according to prudence, here allowing the literal to redound to the moral, there letting the literal remain literal, refusing to strain certain facts or sensory impressions by forcing a supernatural significance upon them.

Insofar as his fiction takes place this side of paradise and above the elevators of hell, his representations will more often instill a sense of mystery than they will unveil the Mysteries. The contemplative realist does not render a wholly Other world so much as he contemplates that unseen Real. Maritain's maxim returns: "Only a mystic can be a complete novelist." Only sanctifying grace, says Father Garrigou-Lagrange, "introduces us into this higher order of truth and life. It is an essentially supernatural life, a participation in the intimate life of God, in the divine nature, since it even now prepares us to see God someday as He sees Himself and to love Him as He loves Himself." Only this grace, which elevates the soul's "vitality and [makes] it bear no longer merely natural fruits but supernatural ones, meritorious acts that merit eternal life for us"—only the Author of this grace (as it was in the beginning, is now, and ever shall be) can make the contemplative realists more vital—and their writings, thereby, more real.

As T.S. Eliot's bird knew well: "Humankind / cannot bear very much reality." Cognizant of the dusty nature of fiction, as well as the limits of human nature, the contemplative realist escalates the spiritual artfully, and when he presences the workings of Spirit he shows that such is the richest reality.

This thought returns us to Fr. Lynch's vision of tragedy as that which elevates us to the consideration of beauty but not by means of beauty. In his commentary on the *Poetics*, Francis Ferguson defines tragedy as an "imitation of an action that is serious, complete, and of a certain magnitude." The action that art aspires to represent is "mainly a psychic energy working outwards." Action, in other words, is not that which is external or outside the soul, but what Dante calls "movement-of-spirit." Still further, Aristotle establishes three species of action: doing, making, and contemplation. Rather than being the antinomy of action, "contemplation is intensely active." It is, Ferguson argues, the highest form of action, that which the tragedy cultivates in its culmination. Take Sophocles' *Oedipus Rex*. In the final lines of the play, the chorus contemplate in Oedipus' self-blinded state "a general truth of the human condition":

> Men of Thebes: look upon Oedipus.
> This is the king who solved the famous riddle
> And towered up, most powerful of men.
> No mortal eyes but looked on him with envy.
> Yet in the end ruin swept over him.
> Let every man in mankind's frailty
> Consider his last day; and let none
> Presume on his good fortune until he find
> Life, at his death, a memory without pain.

The chorus, contends Ferguson, "has attained that mode of action, *theoria*, contemplation of the truth, which Aristotle regarded as the goal of human life."

The contemplative realist aspires after the same end, with the major difference that his definition of what constitutes "serious action" of "a certain magnitude" is informed more by St. Peter's pendulum swing than it is by that of Oedipus. As Elif Batuman implies in her novel *The Idiot*, even the tale of "an American teenager, the world's least interesting and dignified kind of person," is worth telling. On the other hand, contemplative realism regularly extends its canvas beyond the human, reminding us that the cosmos—too often listed as the "least interesting" act in town—is worth narrating too. Take the following from Flannery O'Connor's *Wise Blood* in which her immortal Hazel Motes, stalking in towering indignance (which masks, imperfectly, his desperate flight from his own dignity) down the streets of a city new to him, pretends to be able to ignore this truth—yet all the while O'Connor's controlling intelligence induces us to attend to it:

> His second night in Taulkinham, Hazel Motes walked along down town close to the store fronts but not looking in them. The black sky was underpinned with long silver streaks that looked like scaffolding and depth on depth behind it were thousands of stars that all seemed to be moving very slowly as if they were about some vast construction work that involved the whole order of the universe and would take all time to complete. No one was paying any attention to the sky.

O'Connor's comedy here seems to yearn presciently, prophetically, after Nobel laureate Olga Tokarczuk's dream of a narrative perspective "from where everything can be seen." Such a dream is impossible. God alone reserves such a vantage. But a widening perspective, allowing us intersections and interrelations, affiliations and consequences that a too-narrow telling would miss, in part because seeing so much would restore our sense that we are, as Tokarczuk puts it, "mutually connected to a single whole," which brings with it a "completely different kind of responsibility for the world, because it becomes obvious that every gesture 'here' is connected to a gesture 'there.'" Our realist contemplates these connections with intense interest, singing the contortions and conversions of our bodies and our souls not as an intermediary chorus-like commentator, nor as an objective observer who has ascetically eliminated himself from the picture. He sees them with ardent affection, a lover of his readers and his characters who loves God still more, loves reader and character all the more for seeing both in light of their connection to the "Love that moves the sun and other stars."

The goods of such a way of seeing extend beyond the admittedly circumscribed scope of literary art. On and off the page, be he melancholic artist or monkish human, our realist reaches after the same fragile espial of beauty and goodness. However diminished fiction's significance may be in our time, though, the literary landscape still holds the power to shape visions of what constitutes a good life for human beings—to provide what David Foster Wallace describes as "sources of insight on comparative worth . . . guides to why and how to choose among experiences, fantasies, beliefs, and predilections." As Wallace observes, the collective cultural appetite for such guides may be truthfully argued to ebb low at the moment. Yet there may be hope in the thought that human nature, holding stable despite continual attempts at its reinvention, will eventually sicken of certain proffered nourishments it was never meant to thrive on.

Meanwhile, we must seek our own way forward, leaning, if we like, for support on St. Augustine: "Bad times, hard times: this is what people keep saying: but let us live well, and times shall be good. Such as we are, such are the times." The good that is to have its extensions will first have its incarnations. I have said that the potentialities of contemplative realism, rooted in genealogies of literary realism on the one hand and in nascent contemporary writers' visions on the other, are already well established. Yet a conscious contemplative realist *movement*, to the extent it has begun, still exists only in its earliest nascence. Such as we write, such are the times.

This little *essai* seeks to overturn a few stones: to bespeak a sense of direction for contemplative realists and their fellow travelers; to celebrate fiction's still-glimmering reach even on the edge of our darkening age, and above all to paint a future full of hope, however many horrors may befall us. For the literary artist, this hope takes the utterly concrete, ever-alluring, form of a task not yet finished.

Let's get real. "Man's ability to see is in decline." Our very sense of life, of experience, of interior and exterior sensation, our ability to sort between the specious and the precious—all of this threatened with obscurity on all sides, blinkered by ideologies and technological innovations that promise to provide clear windows but instead function as unreal filters, distorting the mind's rapprochement with reality. Such influences, all the while claiming to expand our vision, radically hamper the soul's depth perception. For the realist, this hampering of the *humane* is itself a story worth telling: the way the various non-convivial tools of the technocracy we inhabit can remake man into something close to a mere moving picture consuming shadows. I think of *Underworld* and *White Noise* by the raised-Catholic novelist Don De Lillo, whose questers seek—amidst an "Airborne Toxic Event" that may not be entirely unfamiliar to us—"to find a kind of radiance in dailiness. Sometimes this radiance can be almost frightening. Other times it can be almost holy or sacred."

To *see clearly* under such circumstances requires continual attentiveness, continual self-correction, continual communal reference to the visions of others similarly engaged. To this end, we wear W.H. Auden's aphorism like a habit: "Among the many qualities required to create or to appreciate art of any style or age, the most necessary of all is an unlimited capacity for reverence and repentance." The relation between vision and will, too complex to admit of full description here, has this implication: that to act well we must first see well. For literary characters and for their creators, distortion of sight breeds distortion of choice; look at us trading our free choice of the will for a proliferation of paralyzing optionalities known all too late to be dead ends.

Learning how to see means, in part, learning how to close one's eyes to so many futile rabbit holes, but it also means learning how to be temperate in appreciating even the beautiful. For if beautiful realities are themselves innately good, we are yet marred by what St. Augustine called "concupiscence of the eyes," a sinful mode of seeing wherein (as Pieper puts it) the eye "does not aim to perceive reality, but to enjoy 'seeing'" in the same way a glutton can overindulge in eating not for nourishment but to titillate the palate. Concupiscence of the eyes, that subspecies of the vice St. Thomas names *curiositas,* can remake the world according to the image of man, especially when (again in Pieper's words) "it surrounds itself with the restlessness of a perpetual moving picture of meaningless shows, and with the literally deafening noise of the impressions and sensations breathlessly rushing past the windows of the senses. Behind the flimsy pomp of its façade dwells absolute nothingness." We grow quickly tired and disinterested in such sights. This tiredness may take the shape of boredom which, says Jean-Luc Marion, "does not have any interest in whatsoever may be, and hence has no more negative interest than positive . . . What does this gaze [of boredom] see? It sees all and nothing, all as nothing, all that is as if it were not." Like the hero of David Foster Wallace's *The Pale King*, the contemplative realist does not settle into boredom as the inevitable mood and mode of a fatigued age. He discovers, rather, how to "deal with boredom. To function effectively in an environment that precludes everything vital and human. To breathe, so to speak, without air. The key is the ability, whether innate or conditioned, to find the other side of the rote, the picayune, the meaningless, the repetitive, the pointlessly complex. To be, in a word, unborable." He does not discard one flimsy pomp for another, but—please God—submits to an asceticism of cognition whereby we train our souls to ascertain the action of Grace in and around the contests of the human spirit.

Though the contemplative realist may only be able to depict this situation after having first fought free *from* it, he will not rest content until he has rendered this relation between strained vision and enslavement, between a more complete seeing and the fullness of choice, knowing that human life is ordered toward other and higher freedom that too many of us would mistake as a restrictive straightjacket. I mean the kind of freedom of will we hope to possess in bliss, when sin will have no power to tempt us. St. Augustine pays homage to this at the end of his *City of God*: "They will be more free than ever—so free, in fact, from all delight in sinning as to find, in not sinning, an unfailing source of joy."

On this side of the beatific vision, the contemplative realist is content to do lowly tasks, sweeping the floor of a decrepit cave to make room for some roofless travelers afoot, spying a glistening black spider on the wall, abdomen bearing a blaring red hour-glass, a dizzying descent in the fullness of time, lit by a star so foreign and here, so faraway near, now follow its spinning dangling above an empty crèche that awaits a King, and sing of the once-golden now-groaning hay and the grime-stained ground three feet away where the lady of Nazareth lays down the Savior and blows and flicks at the beautiful web, sending the black widow far from the baby who God does he cry, does he cry, does he now—he does all of the agony achingly well. Fed by the majestic poverty of the Word he will write another novel of the nameless nobody who happens to be made in the *imago Dei*, numbering the hairs of her head very carefully, surprised to find in her insignificance some of the deepest drama in the cosmos. But daily he must ascend the mountain to be alone and to pray in great silence, moved by St. Bonaventure's promise of what might happen in passive surrender when the soul "embraces with love the Incarnate Word, inasmuch as she receives delight from Him and passes over to Him in ecstatic love, she recovers her sense of taste and touch. Having recovered the spiritual senses, the soul now sees, hears, smells, tastes, and embraces her beloved," capable at last of singing as the bride from the *Canticle of Canticles*, "which was composed for the exercise of contemplation."

ABOUT THE AUTHOR

Joshua Hren is founder of Wiseblood Books and co-founder of the Master of Fine Arts in Creative Writing at the University of St. Thomas, Houston. Joshua regularly publishes essays and poems in such journals as *First Things, America, Public Discourse, Commonweal, National Review, Catholic World Report, New Oxford Review, University Bookman, Law & Liberty,* and *LOGOS.* His books include: the short story collections *This Our Exile* and *In the Wine Press*; the book of poems *Last Things, First Things, & Other Lost Causes*; *Middle-earth and the Return of the Common Good: J.R.R. Tolkien and Political Philosophy*; *How to Read (and Write) Like a Catholic*; and the novel *Infinite Regress.*

Made in the USA
Las Vegas, NV
13 March 2024

87114520R00039